"This is a gem of a book. David Fideler and Sabrineh Fideler have crafted an enticing introduction to some of the greatest mystical poets of Sufism. Highly recommended."

— Jay Kinney, editor of *The Inner West*

"The elegant simplicity of the poems makes them a perfect accompaniment to a meditation practice, as well as a wonderful gift idea."

— *Yogi Times*

"In addition to the richness of the poems themselves, the reader who may be unfamiliar with Persian poetry is given guidance in the book for understanding this type of poetry. The authors provide teaching on understanding Persian poetry in their introduction and helpful endnotes on particular poems, along with a glossary of terms specific to understanding Sufi poetry. Their translations along with the background information provide an amazing introduction for those new to Sufi poetry, and a wonderful resource for those well acquainted with such poetry."

— *Sufism*

"The Fidelers' translations of the poems, many of which have been brought into English for the first time, are superb and lucid throughout, bringing forth the quintessence of quatrains, ghazals, and other forms of this essential yet elusive verse."

— *Rain Taxi Review of Books*

"A wonderful introduction."

— *National Review Network*

LOVE'S
ALCHEMY

LOVE'S ALCHEMY

Poems from the Sufi Tradition

Translated from the Persian by
DAVID AND SABRINEH FIDELER

New World Library
Novato, California

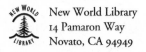 New World Library
14 Pamaron Way
Novato, CA 94949

Interior design by Tona Pearce Myers

Library of Congress Cataloging-in-Publication Data
Love's alchemy : poems from the Sufi tradition / translated by David and Sabrineh Fideler.
    p.   cm.
Includes bibliographical references and index.
ISBN 978-1-57731-535-3 (hardcover : alk. paper)
ISBN 978-1-57731-890-3 (paperback : alk. paper)
1. Sufi poetry, Persian—Translations into English. I. Fideler, David R., 1961– II. Fideler, Sabrineh, 1972–.
PK6449.E5L684 2006
891'.551009—dc22   2005035207

First paperback printing, December 2009
ISBN 978-1-57731-890-3
Printed in the United States on 30% postconsumer-waste recycled paper

g New World Library is a proud member of the Green Press Initiative.

10 9 8 7 6 5 4 3 2 1

Love existed before heaven or earth.
Love's presence is not from our time.

— Ḥāfiẓ

Contents

Introduction

*That which frees you
from your tiny self*

Nowhere has poetry been more prized for its spiritual and artistic value than in the classical Persian world. A devotion to poetry still permeates Persian culture today: the lyrics of traditional music are made up almost entirely of Sufi mystical poetry by such masters as Rūmī and Ḥāfiẓ, and many contemporary Persians have memorized dozens of pages of verse by the great writers. Lines quoted from classical poets appear in ordinary conversation; even street peddlers render their sales pitches into verse. In earlier times, court poets were highly rewarded for their works, and the greatest classical poets were the Sufi mystics, whose beautiful, tranquil tombs are still traveled to by thousands each year, partly because of the spiritual blessing (*baraka*) a pilgrim might acquire by visiting such a holy spot.

In short, the poetry of the classical Sufi writers is very much alive, and still regarded as the highest literary art in Persian culture today. Historically, the rhythm and form of this poetry have been so closely intertwined with music, calligraphy, and even sacred architecture, that at first it is difficult for us Westerners to grasp such a beautifully integrated world—a world in which the arts are so thoroughly harmonized with one another, with daily life, and with the deepest human needs. While these arts are surely meant to inspire delight, they are not forms of "entertainment." All sacred art seeks to open the soul to a direct perception of reality's spiritual dimension.

Over the last twenty years readers in America and Europe have developed a profound thirst for the compelling work of Sufi poet Jalāl al-Dīn Rūmī (1207–1273), which has made Rūmī the best-selling poet in America. Born near the town of Balkh in what is now Afghanistan, Rūmī's native language was Persian. When he was around the age of ten, his family fled the Mongol invaders and ended up in Konya, Turkey, an important town on the silk route, where Rūmī taught and where his tomb is now located. His great teaching-work, the *Mathnawī,* consisting of rhymed couplets, contains twenty-five thousand verses divided into six books, while his *Dīwān* (collected poems) contains some five thousand separate works—over forty thousand verses. Teaching the spiritual power of love and the divine unity at the heart of reality and the world's religious paths, Rūmī has become one of the most treasured voices of spiritual insight in today's world and is by far the best-known Persian poet of all time.

Yet if this volume conveys anything, it is the message that Rūmī is not alone—just an extraordinary representative of a much larger tradition of Persian mystical poetry, which reflects the same themes, the same beauties, the same insights. Persian Sufi poetry is a tradition that spans a thousand years, and in the same way that Rūmī studied and drew on the works of the earlier poets, later poets read and expanded on his work too. But because of the way Rūmī has been presented to modern readers—practically as a lone voice taken out of context—it is easy to overlook the fact that he is part of a living tradition: one that existed before him and continues to the present day.

It is our hope that the works assembled in this collection will help introduce English-speaking readers to the wider tradition that Rūmī represents, to kindred voices who rise to Rūmī's greatness, to other masters of Sufi poetry whose work is cut from the same bolt of spiritual cloth. In order to emphasize the unity of the tradition, we have not arranged the poems either by author, time period, or by theme, but the dates of death of the nearly eighty poets represented here, when they are known, can be located in the index.

With a few exceptions, most of the poems translated here are *rubā'īyāt*, or quatrains: poems only four lines in length, focusing on a central theme or idea. These four-line poems are concise spiritual meditation, or "mystical epigrams," that possess a formal structure akin to that of Japanese haiku. Historically, the *rubā'ī* form was the first type of poetry to be used by Persian mystics. Like the other types of Persian poetry, they were sung or recited with music at Sufi gatherings.

THE LANGUAGE OF
PERSIAN MYSTICAL POETRY

All these poems reflect aspects and teachings of a spiritual tradition—the inner, gnostic, or mystical tradition of Islam—known as Sufism or *taṣawwuf* (purification). But, like Rūmī, these poets do not strictly "belong" to Persia, to the Islamic world, or even to Sufism; like Rūmī, they belong to the entire world, and especially to those readers who taste the essence and grasp the spirit of their work. In the words of one poet, "My place is the placeless / my trace is the traceless." The same could be said of the poetic tradition, for the vision behind these works is ever-living, not bound to a particular people, time, or place.

Persian is a rich, multidimensional language, in which one word can convey a host of meanings and nuances. But the central charm of Persian poetry—and the major stumbling block for noninitiates—is its symbolism. In our modern, secular world, we tend to take things quite literally or at face value; but to the mystics of the world's spiritual traditions everything contains multiple levels of meaning. In sacred texts, the literal dimension often represents just the outermost husk. This is certainly true of Persian mystical poetry, which makes use of a complex, meaning-laden vocabulary from the Sufi tradition. Because of this, even a few lines of poetry can encapsulate an entire world of meaning. To really translate such a work into English may require more words and lines than the original, and some symbols do not "translate" at all but must be understood on their own level.

A large percentage of Persian poetry is written in symbolic code. The reader, in turn, is expected to understand the code in order to grasp the full meaning of the poetry. Deeper still, lurking underneath the symbolic code, lies a vision of the structure of reality, the human condition, and the spiritual path, all of which the symbols allude to. Thus, it is no exaggeration to say that much of the content of Sufi poetry is meant to be understood before you actually read it! While this system presents certain barriers, it also allows the Sufi poets to transmit great depths of meaning, even in a poem of only four lines. It also provides the reader with an ongoing source of delight—for as the reader's understanding continues to expand, the same poems can continue to reveal deeper levels of meaning over the course of many years.

The most common symbols are now well known to many readers: wine, prohibited by Islam, refers to divine love and the mystic knowledge it brings. Intoxication or drunkenness refers to divine inebriation, ecstasy, and direct knowledge of the divine. The Beloved or Friend is a reference to God, but it may simultaneously refer to a human being in whom the qualities of the divine are reflected.

So far, so good, but the symbolism can become intricately complex after that. In some poetry, each aspect of the Beloved's face—downy cheeks, mole, lips, tresses of hair, eyebrows—refers to some aspect of ultimate reality. Other meanings also come into play. The Beloved's tress or strand of hair, for instance, acts as a snare: the curl at the end hooks the lover, drawing him to the Beloved, after which, of course, it is all over! In some works the tress of hair is instead likened to a polo stick. The polo ball is the lover's head, which must be offered up on the earth in sacrifice to the Beloved before it can be firmly whacked into another level of perception.

When you read a poem that refers to the "tavern," you must know in advance that the "Tavern of Ruin" (*kharā-bāt*) is the symbolic gathering place of the Sufis. It is the lonely, unfrequented place on the outskirts of town where wine is served, away from mosques; and it is visited by "rogues" or "profligates"—that is, by Sufis or dervishes. In the Tavern of Ruin you drink wine under the guidance of a master, experience intoxication, and pass away from both the egoism of the false self and the illusions that people take for reality. The Tavern of Ruin is the true Sufi meeting place, where one can experience genuine communion with a deeper level of reality.

The symbol of the Tavern became firmly established in Sufi poetry and illustrates just how complex the poetic code became. In every institutionalized religion there are always some people who act piously and sanctimoniously around others, motivated by a type of spiritual arrogance or egoism rather than by a genuine sense of surrender to the divine. The symbol of the Tavern is the opposite of the mosque and carries a profound meaning. It takes aim at all those individuals — including Sufis — who find in religion a way to inflate their own self-image. The taverngoers, by contrast, are the lowest of the low in their poverty and humility, which makes a genuine type of spirituality possible — one rooted in selflessness. As the poet Ḥāfiẓ puts it,

> Stop acting so holy and putting down the
>   taverngoers!
> Another person's sins will never be tallied by you.
>
> Whether I'm good or bad, mind your own
>   business!
> In the end, everyone reaps what they have sown.
>
> Each person, whether sober or drunk, seeks the
>   Beloved;
> every place is love's home, whether synagogue or
>   mosque.
>
> My head surrenders, lying on the bricks of
>   the tavern's door...
> Stop trying to rob me of heaven's grace.

While most of the poems collected here are fairly straightforward, some require a word of explanation. Notes are provided at the end of the book to explain aspects of the original poems that can't be gracefully brought over in translation, and we have also provided a glossary of symbols and common terms. Appendix 2 describes the *rubā'ī* form in greater depth, and appendix 1 explains the rules we follow when making translations.

LOVE'S ALCHEMY

In the Sufi view, the sun can reveal itself in the atom; the ocean can reveal itself in a single drop; and God can reveal himself in the human beloved. Sufism emphasizes the unity of all existence. Once purified, the human heart becomes a mirror that reflects and knows the light of God. Contrary to the puritanical forms of religion that split off divine presence both from the world and from human life, Sufism celebrates divine nearness and intimacy. Rather than being distant and aloof, God is described as the "Beloved" or the "Friend." Above all, the mystic desires intimacy with God.

In Sufi poetry, we find a conscious blurring of distinctions between human and divine love. They are intertwined. In ecstasy, the human lover loses himself in another; the mystic loses him- or herself in God. The language of love is used by the Sufi poet to express an insatiable longing for divine nearness that would otherwise transcend verbal description.

The very best poems produce a shift in awareness that takes us outside ourselves. In this place, momentarily, time seems to slow down or even to stop. We view life from another perspective—one that seems strangely familiar, and perhaps even more real, than our casual, day-to-day way of looking at things. In this way, by stepping beyond ourselves into the Tavern of Wonder, we catch a glimpse of our true deeper self, and of our true deeper ties.

While these works explore many aspects of the spiritual path, we have chosen the title *Love's Alchemy* to highlight the central Sufi theme of the transformative power of love. As Rūmī pointed out, all types of love are ultimately aspects of our love for God; all kinds of love can lead to God. The constant heat of love's fire allows a soul to fully ripen. It allows an individual who is "raw" or immature to attain a "cooked" or even a "burnt" state. Most important, the power of love allows the individual to surrender the false self of the isolated ego for the sake of the Beloved and receive a deeper vision of reality—a vision that is no longer self-centered. In the words of Fakhr al-Dīn 'Irāqī,

> The first step in love
> is losing your head.
>
> After the petty ego
> you then give up your life
> and bear the calamity.
>
> With this behind you, proceed:
> Polish the ego's rust
> from the mirror
> of your self.

And as Khāqānī Shirwānī writes,

It is love that speaks to you,
calling you beyond the limits
of this created realm.

That which frees you
from your tiny self
also is love.

For the Sufis the highest form of knowledge is a kind of love, and the highest form of love is a type of direct knowing, or *gnōsis*. Yet the false self, with its petty egoism and socially conditioned responses, presents an overwhelming obstacle that isolates the soul from a genuine vision of Reality and the presence of the Beloved—whether the beloved is God or another human being. As Rūmī advises, "If you want to know your *self*, come out of yourself / Leave the tributary and flow toward the River." Or as another classical writer puts it, "Know that when you learn to lose yourself, you will reach the Beloved. There is no other secret to be learnt, and more than this is not known to me."

Put in psychological terms, it is the self-absorbed narcissism of the modern self that keeps us trapped in a tiny, lonely bubble of isolated awareness, unable to hear and participate in the larger choir of creation. While actively marketed as a healthy model of human existence, this isolation from others—and from the greater, living world in which we are embodied—constitutes a primary root of our modern spiritual, social, and ecological dilemmas.

As the Sufis clearly realized, love alone possesses the power to lead us beyond ourselves—and enables us to make the types of liberating personal sacrifices that might not otherwise be possible. For this reason, the spiritual opportunities present in love must never be overlooked if we wish to become the fully human individuals we are meant to be.

LOVE'S
ALCHEMY

INVISIBLE CARAVANS

Love's concert is calling,
but the flute can't be seen.

The drunks are in sight,
but the wine can't be seen.

Hundreds
of caravans
have passed
this very way—

Don't be surprised
if their trace can't be seen.

Muḥammad Shīrīn Maghribī

BLOOM LIKE A ROSE

Your heartrending fire
made me bloom like a rose.

I died at your feet
and returned fast to life.

My inborn freedom
offered nothing in profit;
but now I am free,
since becoming your slave.

Sanā'ī

THE SAME LANGUAGE

To speak the same language
is kinship and affinity,
yet a person stuck with those
he can't confide in
is trapped like a prisoner
enchained by lack of understanding.

It is, indeed, ironic:
There are many people
from India and Turkey
who speak the same language,
while there are countless Turks
who really can't understand one another.

The universal language is authentic insight.

To be one in heart is surely superior
to only speaking the same words.

Rūmī

DROWNED IN YOUR ESSENCE

All the world's atoms
are really your mirrors,
drowned in your essence
like drops in the sea.

Like waves that roll over,
crashing in emptiness,

they deny themselves—

they offer your proof.

Wālah Dāghistānī

STONE HEARTS

Woe to that heart
who cannot sense
the beauty in music!

Never waste your time
discussing love's ways
with a stone heart.

Strangers to love
are not invited
to the Spiritual Concert.

Only those who burn
will give off smoke.

Saʿdī

Four Elements

Within your nature
is every element,
so listen to
some sage advice:

You are demon
and wild beast
and angel
and human—

Whatever you cultivate,
that you will be.

Bābā Afḍal Kāshānī

Your Irresistible Glance

With your irresistible glance,
you captured my heart and soul.

Having robbed me of those,
take away my name and accomplishments too.

If any trace of me remains in this world,
please, don't delay—take that too.

'Ayn al-Quḍāt Hamadānī

STILL HANGING ON

As long as a speck of your existence still remains,
the thought of idolatry still remains too.

You said, "I broke the idol of imagination,
so now I am free" —

But that idol
you supposedly demolished
is still hanging on.

Saʿdī

ATTACHMENT

Whoever's chained to the world
suffers more.

Whoever's free of attachment,
like a dervish,
suffers less.

A donkey with a louder bell
always attracts a heavier load.

Abū Saʿīd Abī 'l-Khayr

BACK TO LIFE

Whoever you embrace
will have everlasting life.

Those drawn to your thought
will dwell in happy fields.

If you pass by one
who fell on love's sword—
your footsteps
will bring him
back to life.

Khwājū Kirmānī

THE GLOW OF YOUR PRESENCE

Where have you taken your sweet song?
Come back and play me a tune.

I never really cared for the things of this world.
It was the glow of your presence
that filled it with beauty.

Ḥāfiẓ

EVERY DIRECTION

When traveling
love's pathway,
never stop
turning your soul
toward the eternal sun.

But since the Real
shines forth
from every direction,
why aim your prayers
at only one spot?

Fayḍ Fayyāḍī

WITHOUT HINDRANCE

When the morning of friendship with God begins
    to dawn,
the soul becomes distant from the entire world.

You then reach a place in which each breath of the
    soul,
without the eye's hindrance,
can see the Friend.

Sayf al-Dīn Bākharzī

LIFE AND DEATH

When the body dissolves
don't think that it's death.

But ignorance, clearly,
is the death of the soul.

With knowledge
each breath
will give your soul life.

In ignorance
each breath
chips your essence away.

Muḥaqqiq Ardabīlī Bīdgulī

THE PATHWAY FINALLY OPENED

When my heart came to rule
in the world of love,
it was freed
from both belief
and from disbelief.

On this journey,
I found the problem
to be myself.

When I went beyond myself,
the pathway finally opened.

Mahsatī Ganja'ī

THE KING'S ROYAL FALCON

When I drew near
to the candle of your face,
I became plaintive and daring,
just like the moth.

On the day I'm released
from this miserable cage,
like the king's royal falcon
I'll fly free at last.

Khwāja 'Abdallāh Anṣārī

ASLEEP

When I became water,
I looked like a mirage.

When I became the sea,
I looked like froth
and foam.

When I became aware,
the entire world
seemed forgetful.

When I became awake,
I saw I'd been asleep.

Bīnawā Badakhshānī

THE SOUL'S FREEDOM

When a person of heart speaks, why say
    they're wrong?
If you lack eloquence,
why quarrel with words, anyway?

Here's the real problem, as I see it—
I can't worship this world or the next.
Thank God for the soul's freedom.

Ḥāfiẓ

THE SUFI'S CAP

What's the use
of those woolen robes
and the Sufi's cloak?

Forget the attire
and make yourself free
of blameworthy deeds!

Wearing a woolen hat
won't make you a Sufi.

Be humble like a dervish—
then you can wear
any cap that you please.

Sa'dī

ESSENCE AND FORM

We've lost the essence
and worship the husk.

But who wants the shell
without tasting the nut?

Seduced by the form,
we're not really alive—

Regaining the essence,
we've become life itself.

Sanā'ī

YOUR HEART

Your heart is the mirror
of the essence most high.

Of the king's royal mint
your heart is the prize.

The heart's a vast ocean—
but only holds
a single pearl.

If I want such a treasure,
your heart I am seeking.

Shāh Ni'matallāh Walī

Coming Clean

We placed the prayer carpet
on the wine jar
and made ablutions
with the tavern's dust.

Perhaps in these taverns
we've rediscovered that life—
the one we lost
in the seminary.

Abū Ḥāmid Muḥammad Ghazālī

The Greatest Name

We are the Treasure
whose spell is the world.

We are that Essence
molded into
human form.

If you are seeking out
the Greatest Name,
don't pass us by—

Don't forget,
we are that name.

Muḥammad Shīrīn Maghribī

FINDING LIFE

True love is nothing but drinking the wine of
   eternity.

In this state, the soul finds life only by dying—
but I wanted things in reverse!

I thought, "*First* I will know you, *then* I will die."
He replied, "Whoever knows me never dies."

Rūmī

Hidden Treasure

Topple the ego to find yourself.

Why worry about the stars
when you are your sky?

The world is full of obvious things,
but you—
you're a hidden treasure.

Remember with joy, you are your world.

Sanā'ī

Reality and Appearance

You who search
the way of love:

In your mind,
you seem to think
you are praying to God—

But one who truly worships the Beloved
never engages
in self-worship.

There is a difference
between real love
and the love of appearances.

Shāh Abū 'Alī Qalandar

HUNDREDS OF WAYS

Today, like every day,
we are ruined and lonely.

Don't retreat,
fleeing your emptiness
through the doorway
of thinking.

Try making some music instead.

There are hundreds of ways
to kneel in prayer—
hundreds of ways to open
toward the heart
of the Friend's beauty.

Rūmī

PERPLEXED

Those who went the way
of reason and logic—

And those who mimicked
the conventions of learning,
the dogmas of faith—

They never came to know
the secrets of existence.

They became perplexed
in the world
and left perplexed too.

Ṣafī 'Alī Shāh

FAR AWAY

Those who dwell
in the Beloved's presence
don't obsess on his thought
and speak of him
even less—

But those who huff and howl
like the bellows of a bagpipe,
call for him in a loud voice
because they are far away.

Bābā Afḍal Kāshānī

A MIRAGE

The world is a veil
on the face of our Friend.

The world is a bubble
in the sea of his existence.

In the sight of those greedy for the Water of Being,
the world is a mirage in the desert of seeking.

Muḥammad Shīrīn Maghribī

THE WIND AT DAWN

The wind at dawn
is the soul's confidant.

Don't find yourself asleep.

This is the time to share
your greatest need.

Don't find yourself asleep.

From before-the-beginning to beyond-the-last,
the two eternities are present now.

Don't find yourself asleep.

The door of the two worlds
is open now.

Don't find yourself asleep.

Rūmī

Not What We Thought

The way of union
is not what we thought.

The world of soul
is not what we imagined.

The Fountain of Eternal Life
is closer than you think.

The Water of Life
is in this very house—
but still, we need to drink it.

Ṣadr al-Dīn Qunawī

The Gift of Life

The thought of you made me homeless—
but loving you gave me eternal life.

Your grace and generosity made my body like a
soul.

In this realm of endless toil, nothing could be finer
than this.

Sanā'ī

THE SCENT

Today I feel trapped,
tightly bound
in the cage of existence.

I need the scent
of nonbeing
to set me free.

Just for a moment,
lend me the polish
of grace:

Scour the rust of being
from the mirror
of my true Reality.

Shihāb al-Dīn Yaḥyā Suhrawardī

ONE AND MANY

The Sun's shining essence
is always just one;
but its rays spread out
and show it as "many."

Each created thing
is like a colored lamp
of the Sun—

The essence is one,
but the attributes many.

Ibn Muḥammad Hādī Riḍā Qulī Hidāyat

REMEMBER THE TRUTH

The soul is love and affection—
so know the soul.

But the Truth is ecstasy, forgetting your self.

When "I" and "you" are present,
you're thinking from
the ego's place.

If you hear those two words,
then remember the Truth.

Ṣaghīr Iṣfahānī

THIS SORROW

The sorrow
of his love
should become
your habit.

Then you'll discover
his love is sweet.

Act like a human being
and embrace this sorrow—

In the end
you will see
this love
is He.

Majd al-Dīn Ṭāliba

EVERY FACE TURNS TOWARD YOU

You show your face
in every particle.

You've become
the shining sun
from every direction.

Present in Ka'ba and present in monastery,
every face
turns toward your own—

You are the destination
of believers
and nonbelievers
alike.

Ṭabīb Shīrāzī

Their Number Is Few

The sea is full of pearls,
but the number
of pearl-divers
is few.

The world is full of music,
but the number
of dancers
is few.

Now I'm afraid
that no prayer
will be answered—
since those
who pray truly
are really quite few.

'Imād al-Din Faqīh Kirmānī

TAVERN DWELLERS

The pure-hearted Sufis no longer care to exist—
they're free of compulsion
and no longer worship the self.

They offer their toasts in the Tavern of Ruin—

They're quaffing down wine,
but never get drunk.

Shāh Ni'matallāh Walī

KNOWLEDGE

The path of knowledge
I traveled intensely.

In the circle of mystics
I have been elevated.

But unveiling the heart
I finally came to see—
really—
that I know nothing.

Khwāja Nāṣīr al-Dīn Ṭūsī

Birds of His Sky

The men of His way
breathe from another soul.

The birds of His sky
fly from another nest.

Don't think
you can see them
using *this* sight—

They are beyond
the two worlds
and in another.

Najm al-Dīn Dāya Rāzī

LOVE'S WITNESS

The holy warrior is out hunting for martyrdom;
but the martyr of love, his station is higher.

How could these two ever be the same,
come the Day of Judgment?

The first is killed by the enemy,
but the second is slain by the Friend.

Abū Saʿīd Abī 'l-Khayr

The Hidden Sun

The heavenly spheres
have lost their way
in your amazement.

Bewildered and wondering,
they forever turn
before your door.

You are the hidden sun,
shining in the soul's midst—

Yet who
has seen
such a hidden sun?

'Aṭṭār

The Heart's House

The heart's house that remains unlit
by the divine Sun's majestic rays
is narrow and dark
like an orphan's cell
far away
from the feast
of the Living King.

Such a heart lacks the Sun's radiance:
    Its space does not expand
    Its doors do not open
    There is not even room to breathe.

A constrained grave is more comforting than
    this—
So come, arise from the tomb of your heart.

Rūmī

A Desert

The heart never races—
    except along love's path.

The soul never really begs to speak—
    except the words of love.

Thank God—

You ravaged my heart
    and made it a desert
    so no other love
    can flower there.

Abū Saʿīd Abī 'l-Khayr

LOSING YOUR HEAD

The first step in love
is losing your head.

After the petty ego,
you then give up your life
and bear the calamity.

With this behind you, proceed:
Polish the ego's rust
from the mirror
of your self.

Fakhr al-Dīn 'Irāqī

THE BELOVED'S SCENT

If there is a sign of the Beloved in the idol-temple,
circling the Ka'ba is quite unreasonable.

Without the Beloved's scent, the Ka'ba is just a
house of idols;
but with the Friend's perfume, an idol-temple is
our Ka'ba.

'Ayn al-Quḍāt Hamadānī

HIS LIVING PROOF

The eternal mysteries,
following wisdom's lead,
brought forth
the human form
as their living proof.

As long as the drop
hadn't emerged from the sea,
the ocean
didn't notice
the depths of its splendor.

Mīrza ʿAbd al-Qādir Bīdil

Three Rules

The divine path is nothing but courtesy;
courtesy itself is compassionate action.

As long as you have a soul,
it should be seeking.

Should the entire ocean
be poured in your mouth,
drink a little, but be content.

Khwāja Bāqī Billāh

FIND IT IN YOU

The Divine Book's imprint
is nothing but you.

The mirror of the King's Beauty
is nothing but you.

Not a thing in this world
is outside of you.

Whatever you're seeking—
you'll find it in you.

Bābā Afḍal Kāshānī

LIFT THE VEIL

The day you lift that veil from your face,
you'll hold the entire world hostage.

Reveal your beauty beyond these bounds?
My God—you'll murder every living heart!

Sanā'ī

LEARNING TO BURN

The day love's fire was lit,
the lover learnt
the way of burning
from the Beloved.

This burning and melting
is the Friend's doing—

If the candle were never lit,
the moth would never burn.

Abū Sa'īd Abī 'l-Khayr

RUINED

The curve of your eyebrow
is my only prayer niche.

Your ruby lips
offer the clearest wine.

When the pious saw you,
they prostrated in ecstasy;
the wine-drinkers, too,
became ruined and drunk.

Murshidī Zawwār'ī

THAT WHICH FREES YOU

The bird that sings
pain's song
is love.

The messenger skilled
in the language
of the unseen world
is love.

It is love that speaks to you,
calling you beyond the limits
of this created realm.

That which frees you
from your tiny self
also is love.

Khāqānī Shirwānī

THE BELOVED'S DESIRE

The Beloved wants no lord, no master—
She wants astonishment and devastation!

I'm like a monk, safe in my cloister—

She wants me to give up everything
and roam the world like a dervish!

'Aṭṭār

WITHOUT YOU

Without you,
I have no paradise
and no heaven—

No celestial lake,
no fountain of nectar,
and no sea of life.

With your wrath,
even heaven becomes hell—
but with your grace,
even hell flowers
like springtime.

Saʿd al-Dīn Ḥamawī

SERVICE

Worship is nothing aside
from serving others.

It is not dependent
on prayer rugs, rosaries,
or the Sufi's cloak.

Sa'dī

THE MISSING SUN

You are like the sun—

Come!

Without your face, the garden is yellow and pale—

Come!

Without you, the world is like dust—

Come!

Without you, the circle of love turns cold.

Come!

Rūmī

We Were Together

That idol made us idol-worshipers!

Worse, I think he knows
we can't exist without him.

We were together
sipping wine
on that ancient
Night of Union—

That left us drunk
'til Resurrection's Day.

Awḥad al-Dīn Kirmānī

BEYOND DISTINCTIONS

That fire
whose name is love
burns away
both belief and disbelief.

Belief is one thing—
the religion of love
is something different.

Love's Prophet is beyond race,
beyond creeds,
beyond petty distinctions.

Abū Saʿīd Abī ʾl-Khayr

SEEKING YOUR TRACE

Thanks to you
I'm seeking
the soul of the world.

Bewildered, perplexed—
I seek your presence
in every place.

Now that you've made
a home in my heart,

I'm seeking
your trace
in every space.

Fakhr al-Dīn 'Irāqī

ONLY ONE STEP

Taste the music
in the lover's sigh.

Discover the cure
in yearning's pain.

The distance
to the Beloved
is only one step—

Why not, then,
take that step?

Bahā' al-Dīn Muḥammad 'Āmilī

CHECKMATE

You are the King
and have checkmated
every beautiful soul.

You are the Sun—
the rest are your atoms.

You are the Light—
every creation
is your lamp.

You are the Essence—
the entire world
is your living sign.

Ṭūṭī Hamadānī

Burn Down the House

Take up life in a monastery—
or take up love's fire
and burn down the house.

A monk and a lover
can't live in the same room.

Can't face the truth?

You could always
just
close your eyes.

Sa'dī

TAKE A LOOK THERE

Spend some time with the People of Heart;
in their presence, you'll find a heart too.

If you thirst for the beauty
of the eternal Beloved,
where might you look?

Since your heart is a mirror,
take a look there.

'Abd al-Raḥmān Jāmī

EVEN A WISE EYE

Your names reflect
your boundless essence.

The world displays
your living signs.

The stars trace out
your very proof.

If not enraptured
by your charms, well—
even a wise eye
is truly blind.

Maftūn Hamadānī

WITHOUT NAME, WITHOUT TRACE

Sometimes you secretly
come to the heart.

Sometimes you're seen
before open eyes.

All of these names
and these traces
are yours—

Yet each time you come
without name, without trace.

Muẓaffar Kirmānī

THE VISION OF YOUR FACE

Your love, from before
the beginning of time,
is my soul—
it's my very self.

Your love is the treasure
of my weak, begging heart.

Perhaps your beauty
has been far from me—
but the vision
of your face
has stayed with me always.

Sulṭān Walad

The Mirror and Its Case

Each soul is created to serve as your mirror.

All things in the two worlds
are only your mirrors.

The heart is the mirror of your most royal
    beauty—
and both of these worlds
are the case of that mirror.

Najm al-Dīn Dāya Rāzī

In Mosque and Church

In sanctuary and monastery,
a hundred songs
declare your praise.

You're the clearest light,
but shine forth
in every hue.

Each day and night, your name is called
in Islam's mosque and Europe's church.

Hātif Iṣfahānī

LOST OPPORTUNITY

Seeking life without the Friend's presence,
you didn't spend a moment waiting at love's door.

My God! Sit down and mourn your loss!

That time is gone when you could have been living.

Fakhr al-Dīn 'Irāqī

YOUR LOVE

Religion is nothing
except your love.

Awareness is nothing
except your thought.

Should the world
bring on
a thousand
pains,
I've lost
the knowledge
of your love.

Sayyid Ḥasan Ghaznawī

ACTION

Regardless of how much knowledge
you might acquire,
you are still ignorant
without action—

You would be neither scholar nor learned,
but an animal carrying books.

A donkey doesn't know
whether it's carrying books
or firewood.

Sa'dī

TRADING IN LOVE'S CURRENCY

Reason said, "We live in a world
of six directions—and that's it!"

Love replied, "There is a path beyond,
and I have traveled it many times."

Reason saw a market and set up shop,
but love trades in another currency altogether.

Rūmī

THE BUBBLE

Pass away—
then you'll find
the eternal shore.

To reach the Friend,
you have to go beyond yourself.

One day a bubble
was wondering
about its existence—

When it popped,
it finally
rejoined
the sea.

Fikrī Khurāsānī

THE MIRACLE OF YOUR FACE

Over hundreds of aeons,
creation's fabric
unfolded
until the beauty
of your face
blazed forth
in this world.

From the top of your head
to the tip of your toe,
Subḥānallāh—
All praise belongs to God!

Miraculously,
he has molded you
to my very desire.

Khāqānī Shirwānī

TAKE A GOOD LOOK

One night
during prayers
a vision
of the Beloved
appeared to me.

Lifting the veil
from his face,
he said:

"Take a good look
at the one
you always leave behind."

Awḥad al-Dīn Kirmānī

THE SINGLE PEARL

Once we came to know the Beloved,
we forgot the entire universe.

When we emerged from the broken shell,
we fell in love with the Single Pearl.

Maftūn Hamadānī

THE SUN AND THE SHADOW

Once upon a time
the Beloved came and said:

I possess your love
both day and night—
but you'll never
be my companion
as long as you remain yourself.

I am the Sun,
but you are just a shadow,
walking upon the earth.

Step out of hiding
and walk into my light—
once you've been erased,
then you will be
my closest friend.

'Aṭṭār

WHAT WAS

Once I was here,
but now "I" am not:

If there's really a "me,"
   it could only be you.

If any robe warms
and encompasses me now,
that very robe—
   it could only be you.

In the way of your love,
nothing was left—
neither body nor soul.

If I have any body—
If I have any soul—
then, without question,
   it could only be you.

'Alā' al-Dawla Simnānī

THE SOUL'S DILEMMA

Once again, each day,
I travel the path of your love.

Every night, without fail,
I mourn your absence anew.

My soul lacks the courage
to love one
such as you—
and my heart lacks the strength
to abandon you too.

'Aṭṭār

THIS WAY

On the Friend's pathway
I see neither body nor soul.

Everything but He
is only a dreaming—
or just mere belief.

Every created thing
is far from this way—
if this way, really,
is what I am seeing.

Saḥābī Astarābādī

KA'BA OF THE HEART

On God's pathway
there are two Ka'bas.

One is the Ka'ba you can see;
the other, the Ka'ba of the heart.

As much as you can,
make pilgrimage to the heart—

The heart's value
is greater
than a thousand Ka'bas.

Awḥad al-Dīn Kirmānī

BETWEEN TWO BREATHS

Observe your life, between two breaths.

Breath is a wind, both coming and going.

On this wind you have built your life—
but how will a castle rest on a cloud?

Avicenna (Ibn Sīnā)

PEOPLE OF THE PATH

People of the Path
who know
the secret of meaning
are hidden from the eyes
of the narrow-minded.

Ironically, though,
everyone who comes to know
the divine Reality
possesses the purest faith—
but is labeled an "unbeliever"
by the pious.

Rūmī

DON'T IMAGINE

O wayfarer—
Don't imagine
you're the only one
traveling this path.

Since the Real is everywhere,
don't imagine
he's only in
mosque and monastery.

Don't imagine
that any evil
served up
from the hidden world
is without a share of goodness.

In a word,
if you profess Divine Unity,
don't imagine
any others than He.

Ibn Muḥammad Hādī Riḍā Qulī Hidāyat

DON'T UTTER A SOUND

O nightingale—
Learn love's way
from the moth.

That burnt one
passed away,
but didn't
utter a sound.

These pretenders
are deluded
in seeking him.

Those who came
to know the Friend
never sent back
any news.

Sa'dī

THE MOON OF YOUR LOVE

Not a single soul lacks
a pathway to you.

There's no stone,
no flower—
not a single piece of straw—
lacking your existence.

In every particle of the world,
the moon of your love
causes the heart
of each atom to glow.

Muḥammad Shīrīn Maghribī

Your Generosity

Your generosity offers that which the ocean cannot.
Your kindness is not postponed until tomorrow.

I never needed to ask you for anything.
But who needs to ask the sun for its light?

Rūmī

Every Name That Exists

No atom exists
that is apart
from the sun.

Every raindrop is from
the same ancient sea.

Has no one a name
for this ultimate Truth?

Every name that exists
is already owned
by that Truth.

Dārā Shikūh

SECONDHAND TALK

Never has my idol
shown his face to anyone.

This gossip I'm hearing
is just empty talk.

Even that one
who's singing your praises
has stolen those lines
from somebody else.

Fakhr al-Dīn ʿIrāqī

WHERE WOULD I GO?

Never could my heart
be separate from you—
nor could I worship
anyone else.

If I forget your kindness,
then whom could I love?

If I pass by your street,
then where would I go?

Najm al-Dīn Kubrā

Behind the Veil

Neither you nor I
know the secrets of pre-eternity.

Neither you nor I
have grasped the deepest mystery.

Now we are speaking
beside the veil—

But once that curtain is lifted,
neither you
nor I
will remain.

Abū 'l-Ḥasan Kharaqānī

FREE

My head was full, overflowing with conceit—

I was staggering, drunk—
wasted on the wine
of my imagined greatness.

But your love made me low—
it brought humility.

It freed me
from having
to worship
myself.

'Abd al-Wāsi' Jabalī

YOURS AND MINE

My dear, sanctimonious friends:

The Ka'ba will be yours,
but the idol-temple
will be mine.

The Heavenly Fountain
will be yours,
but the goblet will be mine.

You can have
the finest rosaries;
I'll take the Christian's
lowly cincture.

You can take the
entire world —
but the Beloved
will be mine.

Shaḥna Khurāsānī

THE ARROW

Make your soul the target
of love's arrow
flying from the bow
of the Beloved's hand.

Let it pass through your soul.

Don't bother
to shield yourself
from love's weapon—

Its pathway
through the two worlds
is hidden
even from itself.

'Aṭṭār

Who I Really Am

Make me reject
all things besides you.

Leave me without companion,
without comrade,
and without friend.

First take away the awareness of myself;
then let me see who I really am.

Nashāṭ Iṣfahānī

CREATION MYTH

Made moist with love's dew,
Adam's soil became clay.

A hundred conflicts and tumults
then arose in the world.

The tip of love's sword
glanced the vein
of the spirit—

When one drop emerged,
its name was *the heart*.

Majd al-Dīn Baghdādī

WHAT'S THE USE?

When the heart is full of idolatry,
what's the use
of prostrating your head in prayer?

When poison has already overtaken the body,
what's the use of gulping down medicine?

You'd like to display yourself in public
as a model
of perfect piety—

But what's the use of draping a clean robe
over a dirty soul?

Mahsatī Ganja'ī

Hidden Pearls

Love may cut you deeply—
but like an oyster's shell
it contains
hidden pearls.

Love's burden is great,
but always be willing
to carry this weight.

Like a heavy, laden branch,
it will offer
many fruits.

Raḍī Ghaznawī

Every Place Is Love's Home

In the end, everyone reaps what they have sown.

Each person, whether sober or drunk, seeks the
    Beloved;
every place is love's home, whether synagogue or
    mosque.

Ḥāfiẓ

LIFE'S FLAME

Love is a source of many great troubles.

But lacking love
is a disgrace
for travelers upon this path.

Love is the life force of the entire universe—
those who lack love
are already dead.

Awḥad al-Dīn Kirmānī

BURNT

Love burned up
my very soul.

I learned burning
and melting,
just like the moth.

If my ashes
someday
should be scattered
in hell—
then hell, like me,
would learn
how to burn.

Qīrī Baghdādī

LOOK

Look!

The heart is the truth's kernel;
the body's the shell—

Look!

The face of the Friend
adorns the robe of the soul—

Each atom displays a trace
of His being—

Look!

Is the sunbeam His light—
or is it He Himself?

Shāh Ni'matallāh Walī

THE SECRET IS HIDDEN

Look at the world:
the Divine Secret is hidden.

Like the Fountain of Life,
it's hidden in darkness.

Millions of fish
appeared in the sea—

Because of their number,
the sea went into hiding.

Abū Saʿīd Abī 'l-Khayr

LEADING EVEN FROM HERE

Last night in the wine house
I met a drunken ascetic;
he was wearing a rosary,
with wine cup in hand.

"Why make your home here,
in the Tavern?" I asked.

He answered back—

"There's a pathway to God
leading even from here."

Bahā' al-Dīn 'Āmilī

A Prayer

Keep me
from wanting
this world
or the next.

Crown me
with honor—
please empty
my soul.

Make me
your confidant
on the pathway
of seeking.

Keep me
from taking
any pathway
but yours.

'Abd al-Raḥmān Jāmī

ONE BREATH

It's only one breath
from disbelief's world
to the place
where faith resides.

It's only one sigh
from doubt's waystation
to the homeland of certainty.

Don't now despise
this single, dear breath—
the purpose of life
is just this breath.

Shāh Niʿmatallāh Walī

DUST ON YOUR DOORSTEP

In your service I'm emptied, emptied of myself.
My soul is just the dust on your doorstep.
But I don't offer my heart's gold to just anyone—
The door to this treasure bears only your name.

Ḥāfiẓ

CELEBRATE THIS LOSS

In the land of love
there's no reason
for comfort.

There, everything is loss—
not increase.

But without pain and grief,
how could the cure
ever arrive?

Without error,
how hope
for forgiveness?

Abū Saʿīd Abī 'l-Khayr

ONE AND THE SAME

In the circle of existence
everything, really,
is one and the same.

Being and nonbeing:
one and the same.

Don't think that
lover and beloved
are truly separate:

Witness and witnessed
are one and the same.

Ghayrat Nāyīnī

SEEING

In suffering and pain, I always see the cure.
In wrath and injustice, I see grace and loyalty.

On this earth,
under the roof of the starry sky,
in everything I see,
there I see you.

Sulṭān Walad

YOUR GLANCE

The heart's in love
with your beautiful,
drunken glance.

You are the candle—
the entire world is your fluttering moth.

Our souls, our hearts—
you made them crazy with love.

You quickly became the home of our hearts—
and our hearts, now, are also your home.

Qāsim Anwār

ANOTHER KIND OF RECKONING

In love's tavern, there's another kind of wine.

But for those who adore religion,
they're playing a different game.

Your drunks are free
from the Day of Judgment;
they face
another kind of reckoning
altogether.

Shams al-Dīn Kirmānī

DON'T FLEE

In love's slaughterhouse
only the pure
are ever at risk.

The arrogant and devious
are never prized or desired.

If your heart is pure,
then never flee
the butcher's knife.

Whoever won't be killed
is already dead meat.

Sarmad

SEEKING YOU TOO

In love's meeting place,
on the very first day,
a person of heart
spoke with true promise:

O Seeker!
Don't seek out anyone
who's looking
for someone
who's other than you —

Seek out that one
who is seeking you too.

Ṭālib Jājaramī

SOMETHING DIFFERENT

In love's circle there's another kind of serenity;
in love's wine, another kind of hangover.
What you learned in school is one thing—
love is something entirely different.

Rūmī

A Thousand Eyes

In love,
your lips should be silent.

Inside the heart,
you cook, boil, and burn.

No longer should you have
a single eye—
but you
become
a thousand eyes.

No longer should you have
a single ear—
but you
become
a thousand ears.

Mushtāq Iṣfahānī

FROM YOU

In everything, there's a different gift of your beauty.
In every page of your goodness,
there's a different ecstasy
to be found.

Every defect receives another kind of your perfection.
Every lover finds a different type of union with you.

'Aṭṭār

As You Please

In both fortune
and misfortune
there is always
decline.

Don't complain
if he has put dregs
in your clear wine.

Since the world
is always shifting
and never stays
in the same place,
have a joyful heart
and pass the time
as you please.

Shams Shīrāzī

WHERE'S THE WATER?

In a vision I asked
the Master of Wisdom:

"Can you explain to me
the Names, Attributes,
and Essence
of the Lord of lords?"

He replied:

"You're just like a fish
asking the waves and the bubbles,
Can you show me the way to the water?"

Maftūn Hamadānī

ACHIEVE THE STATE

If you're serious
about joining
the people of vision
you must move from speech
to the inner state.

You won't become one
just by chanting "Unity" —

Repeating the word *sugar*
won't make your mouth sweet.

Dārā Shikūh

A World of Difference

If you're feeling holier than thou,
don't look down
on our lowly station
from your exalted place.

Our existence
has gone the way
of nonexistence.

We are drunk on affection,
but you are drunk on pride.

There's a world of difference
between your intoxication
and ours.

Fayḍī Turbatī

Seeing with Intimacy

If you dwell with the Friend
in genuine intimacy,
then, in the whole world,
you will see
the incomparable God.

Since the whole world
is the living mirror of God,
it is impossible to see anything
aside from God.

Saʿd al-Dīn Ḥamawī

BURNT HEARTS

If you haven't
been touched
by love's burning flame,
how could our hearts
ever really be close?

But if your heart *isn't* burnt,
maybe it's best
to just stay away—

We set fire
to every heart
that hasn't been cooked.

Amīr Khusraw Dihlawī

Drown in Love

If you drown in love, you will taste eternity;
in reason alone, you forsake true life.

Taste the strangeness of this wine!
Love's intoxication is the path to sobriety.

'Ayn al-Quḍāt Hamadānī

Every Atom

If the veil would fall from the Beloved's face,
every atom would dance
like it's stark raving mad.

Every universe is drunk from love's cup—
but the cup is still full,
right to the brim.

'Andalīb Kāshānī

WHAT POSSIBLE USE?

If the heart rides on love's steed,
all its desires will be answered.

But if there were no heart
on which love could settle—

and if there were no love to begin with—

what possible use
could the heart
ever have?

Sa'd al-Dīn Ḥamawī

THE MIRROR AND THE SUN

If the heart doesn't travel
the way of your union,
what should the heart do?

If the soul doesn't long
to be one with the Friend,
what should the soul do?

When the sun's shining glory
blazes forth in the mirror—

If the mirror doesn't say,
"Now look, I'm the sun,"
tell me, then—
what should the mirror do?

Abū Ḥāmid Muḥammad Ghazālī

FACES

If someone's always been steeped
in the presence of God,
for such a soul
the king is like a beggar,
and the beggar is like a king.

In the faces of people,
such a saint
sees God's light.

Yes — *Human beings
are the face of God.*

Kāhī Kābulī

Take a Closer Look

If He is in sight wherever you look,
why cast a blind eye
when it comes to yourself?

The Real said to you
I'm wherever you turn—

So why don't you take
a closer look at yourself?

Dārā Shikūh

WINE WORSHIPER

I always want wine, but never get drunk;
There's nothing I long for, aside from that cup.

But what does it mean to worship this wine?

It means
I can't worship
the ego
like you.

Kamāl al-Dīn Ismaʿīl

Beyond Rite and Ritual

I will pass beyond belief and religion
because your love is higher.

How long can I keep this love a secret?
My only love is you, beyond rite and ritual.

'Ayn al-Quḍāt Hamadānī

THE WORLD-VIEWING CUP

I searched each land
for the world-viewing cup.

I couldn't rest
either day or night.

But when my teacher
finally helped me to see,
I discovered
at last
I am that cup.

Zayn al-Dīn Nasawī

HIDDEN AWAY

I haven't seen your rose garden
in a very long time—

Nor your half-drunk
languishing
narcissus eyes.

You've hidden yourself away
from humanity
like truth—

We haven't seen your face
in a very long time.

Rūmī

WHOLLY UNIQUE

I asked, "Who are you like
in your overwhelming beauty?"

He replied, "Only myself,
as I am quite unique."

*I am love, lover,
and the Beloved.*

*I am Beauty, I'm the mirror,
and the longing eye.*

Abū Saʿīd Abī 'l-Khayr

KEEP ME FREE

I am God's drunk—
forget the wine and the cup.

I'm the hunter's prey—
so let's sell the farm.

Ka'ba and idol-temple
exist only for You—

If not, keep me free
from any such place.

Khwāja 'Abdallāh Anṣārī

YOUR ANCIENT FRIEND

Hidden secrets
are the jewels
of your treasury.

Hidden or seen—
everything springs
from your chest.

Both worlds
were created
only for you.

Heaven's sphere
is your ancient friend.

Maftūn Hamadānī

EMPTINESS

For someone whose trade is emptiness
and whose work is annihilation,
the search for certainty, knowledge,
and religion
has come to an end.

Since he's annihilated,
only God remains—
just God.

This is the meaning of
"when poverty becomes complete,
you find God."

Abū Sa'īd Abī 'l-Khayr

TOUCHED BY YOUR GRACE

Every soul rejoices
if touched by your grace.

Tasting your favor
is eternal good fortune.

When your grace touched an atom
for only a moment,
that atom blazed brighter
than a thousand suns.

Majd al-Dīn Baghdādī

It Would Be Me

Drunk on love's wine?
That would be me.

Broke a thousand vows?
That would be me.

Crazy yet learned—
Scoundrel yet saint—

If anyone is like that
it would be me.

Pūr Bahā Jāmī

Silence

Drink the wine of mystic knowledge,
but don't then forget to keep your lips closed.

It's never a good time
to sell the Divine Secret!

Should you face any troubles,
don't babble and gush
like the mountain spring.

If you remain silent,
you'll then become the sea.

'Aṭṭār

Just Stop

Don't regret the past;
release your worries
about the future.

Don't think about yourself—
and stop trying not to!

Now's the time
to leave the shore—
the Ocean of Unity
is calling...

don't listen...
don't see...

don't say...
don't think...

don't be...

JUST STOP.

Bābā Afḍal Kāshānī

NEVER LOSE THE WAY

Don't lose the trail
of wisdom's scent.

While on this hunt,
don't go astray,
worrying if every little thing
is good or bad.

You are the traveler,
you are the path,
and you are the destination.

Be careful
never
to lose
the way to yourself.

Shihāb al-Dīn Yaḥyā Suhrawardī

BLIND AS A BAT

Divine Oneness
is like being in sunshine.

So why be afraid
of the bat-natured ones?

If they're the cause of your worry,
come out of hiding—

There's no need to run
from those who can't see.

Saḥābī Astarābādī

Lost in Celebration

Do not join us without a tambourine—
we are lost in celebration.

Stand up and beat the drum—
we are now victorious in love!

We are drunk without a drop of wine.
We are beyond anything you have ever imagined.

Rūmī

PATHWAYS

Don't be foolish and think the heart is just inside
    the breast—
or that you will reach the destination with only
    two steps.

Knowledge, piety, asceticism, desire, and seeking—
these are all pathways, but never the final goal.

Bābā Afḍal Kāshānī

NOURISH THE SOUL

Desire the loaf
which nourishes the soul.

Seek the knowledge
which can never
be written
in words.

Desire the secret
hidden in the hearts
of God's friends,
even beyond the grasp
of angels.

Rūmī

What I Ask

Dear God—
I'm only a beggar.

Yet what I ask
is more
than a thousand kings
can ask.

Everyone asks
for something
from your royal threshold—
but I have come
to ask
only *for you*.

Sayyid Ḥasan Ghaznawī

THIS SIDESHOW

Dear Beloved—

How long
will this separation
go on?

Since I am you,
how long
is this "being you"
and "being me"
going to last?

With your jealous nature,
nobody else
even has a chance—
but how long
must I endure this sideshow
with everyone else?

'Azīz Kāshānī

YOUR DISHEVELED CURLS

Dangle a tress from your disheveled curls
and you'll evict the monks from their monasteries.

Shine a reflection of your face in this world
and even the idols will kneel down in prostration.

Rūzbihān Baqlī

SIT BY ME

Come and touch
the Sufi's heart.

If you're like salt,
come lie upon my wounds.

Through your absence,
my heart became a rose garden.

Just for a moment,
sit by the one you've slain.

Khalīl Ṭālaqānī

WITHOUT YOUR PRESENCE

Carrying your thought, why would I think of wine?
Keep the wine-vat sealed—the tavern's now in ruins.
Even heaven's wine, just throw it out.

Without your presence,
even the sweetest drink
is nothing but torture.

Ḥāfiẓ

BEGGING FOR A GLIMPSE

Both worlds are aglow
from the light of the Friend.

You hide in the world
like the soul in a body.

With yearning we wait,
begging
for a glimpse
of your beautiful Oneness—

Please drop all those veils
from the sun of your face.

Shāh Abū 'Alī Qalandar

Arguments of the Wise

Books and reading
don't make up
the Beloved's path.

Reason doesn't lead
to the Plain of Truth.

In the Land of Knowledge,
the arguments of the wise
are like well-worn pathways—
muddy trails
left behind
by wild beasts.

Ḥusayn Muʾmin Yazdī

SINCE THAT DAY

Before diffusing the light
of the Pleiades...

Before stretching
the zodiac's band
across the very heavens...

From before
the beginning
of time...

Since that day,
like a flame upon a candle,
your love's
been bound to us
with a thousand chains.

Najm al-Dīn Dāya Rāzī

Sweep Out the Stable

Be watchful—the grace of God appears suddenly.
It comes without warning to an open heart.

Sweep out the stable of your existence
and the king will gladly enter.

Rūmī

CREATION'S WITNESS

At time's beginning
that beauty
which polished creation's mirror
caressed every atom
with a hundred thousand suns.

But this glory
was never witnessed.

When the human eye emerged,
only then was He known.

Mīrzā 'Abd al-Qādir Bīdil

SWEPT AWAY

At first, the way of your love
seemed easy.

I thought I'd reach
your union
with speed.

After taking a few steps,
I found
the way
is an ocean.

When I stepped in,
a wave swept me away.

Awḥad al-Dīn Kirmānī

IDOL WORSHIP

Since nonexistence
holds the place of honor,
stop all the focus
on yourself.

Existence is your idol,
so decrease your idol-worship.

When you become free
from both being
and nonbeing,
then drink the wine of joy—
but reduce
your drunkenness
on the world.

Aḥmad Jāmī

THE RUST OF STRANGERS

Any heart who resides
in the Beloved's alley
becomes a confidant
of the Court of Secrets.

File away
the rust of strangers
from the heart's mirror;
then it will deserve
the splendor
of the Friend's face.

Gulzār Iṣfahānī

NEARNESS

Although we're near,
you'd never know it.

Thinking of yourself,
our distance
is all
your doing.

Want to reach me?
Then lose yourself.

Walking love's path,
you're either you
or me.

Sanā'ī

KERNEL AND THE SHELL

Although both worlds are only His being,
how did the human become the kernel?
How did the world become the shell?

Is it because
the human
is the pupil of his eye?

Or is it because
the human is the mirror
of the Friend's face?

Muḥammad Shīrīn Maghribī

ONE BODY

All human beings
are the members
of one body—
every person is a glint,
shining from a single gem.

When the world causes pain for one member,
how could the other members
ever rest in peace?

If you lack grief
for another one's sorrow,
why call yourself
a human being?

Sa'dī

LOVE'S ALCHEMY

Abandon the copper of existence
like one who walks the Path—

When you find love's alchemy,
then all will turn to gold.

Sleeping and eating
have drawn you far
from dignity—
when you awake,
you'll recall your true self.

Ḥāfiẓ

TURN WITH THE STARS

If you are seeking your *self,*
come out of yourself.

Leave the tributary
and flow toward the River.

Why carry the burden
of heaven's millstone
when you could turn instead
with the choir
of the circling stars?

Rūmī

DAZED

A person made dazed
by the cup of love
forgets all other joys.

He speaks with remembrance
in his innermost soul—
and then falls silent
to outer disputes.

'Alā' al-Dawla Simnānī

CLEAR WINE

A mystic is one
who passes away —

He abides in the essence
of that which is Real.

Such a person is pure,
clear wine without dregs.

Now whole, he displays
the Most Beautiful Names.

Bīnawā Badakhshānī

SOMETHING ELSE

In love's battlefield,
there's another kind of combat.
There's another kind of victory,
another kind of escape.

All those things you hear—
people crying out,
lamentations,
weeping,
moaning,
and sighing—
are only the sounds
of raw desire.

Love itself
is something else.

Wālah Dāghistānī

BE LIKE THE OCEAN

A falling stone doesn't trouble the ocean.
A mystic who's offended
is still a shallow puddle.

If you are slighted, then bear it with patience.
Through forgiveness, your soul will be pure.

At some point
you'll be nothing but dust;
in humility, become dust today.

Sa'dī

THE CIRCLE

You are the pain
and the cure
of the suffering heart.

You are the lover, love,
and Beloved.

You are the center,
the circle,
the compass that unites.

You are standing apart
from any veil.

Ḥazīn Lāhījī

Translating Persian Poetry

Most popular translations of Rūmī into English have been made without careful reference to the Persian text of the originals, and many are actually adaptations of literal, dry-sounding English-language translations made decades ago by scholars. While these adaptations or "English-to-English translations" are often beautiful, distortions arise, and meanings present in the original poems often become lost in the process.

The word *translation* means "to carry across" and is never just a mechanical undertaking, but an art, especially in the case of poetry. Regardless of a translator's approach, it is simply not possible to produce a literal translation of a poem from Persian—or from any other language—and have it automatically "work" in English.

All our translations are made directly from the Persian text, and we follow three basic rules that we hope allow the original works to be carried over gracefully into modern English:

1. The translation must work in English as a poem (or as an epigram, in the case of quatrains).

2. Rephrasing a line is permitted, if doing so helps to transmit the meaning more clearly.

3. Otherwise, each translation is kept as literal as possible.

Following this method allows us to remain faithful to the ideas and meanings of the original poems, while granting enough freedom to produce good translations.

To illustrate how this method shapes our work, compare our version of a famous Rūmī quatrain to a strictly literal translation:

Literal translation:

> Today, like every day, we are ruined—ruined.
> Don't open the door of thinking; pick up a lute.
> There are a hundred kinds of prayer (*nāmāz*),
>   bowing (*rukū'*), and prostration (*sujūd*)
> for the one whose prayer niche (*miḥrāb*) is the
>   beauty of the Friend.

Our translation:

> Today, like every day,
> we are ruined and lonely.
>
> Don't retreat,
> fleeing your emptiness
> through the doorway
> of thinking.
>
> Try making some music instead.
>
> There are hundreds of ways
> to kneel in prayer—
> hundreds of ways to open
> toward the heart
> of the Friend's beauty.

While the literal translation would work well in an academic study, as Robert Frost once noted, it's the poetry that gets lost in the translation. Because of the numerous technical references in the last two lines, such a literal version does not really work as a poem for English-speaking readers; it also lacks a lyrical sense of rhythm that knits the work together into a whole.

Our translation maintains the sense of the original poem but also works in English. It maintains Rūmī's reference to the practice of prayer, and alludes to the opening of the heart-shaped prayer-niche (*miḥrāb*) in Rūmī's original. While preserving this fidelity, the translation also works for the general reader who is not versed in the intricacies of the Islamic ritual prayer. Finally, in poems like this with meanings or technical terms that cannot be gracefully carried over into English, we provide notes for readers who'd like to go deeper into the Persian text.

MUSIC, STRUCTURE, AND VERSE

Rubāʿī literally means a poem of four lines—a quatrain. In the original Persian, each four-line poem possesses a rhythm and a rhyme scheme. Like the poetry of other cultures, Persian poetry has a musical dimension in its very structure. Mystical and spiritual poetry was often sung or recited with musical accompaniment at Sufi gatherings. To highlight this dimension, a *rubāʿī* is sometimes called a *tarāna,* a "song" or "melody." Even without musical accompaniment—or an English-language translation—hearing a poem recited in Persian is a sonorous, magical experience.

Unfortunately, it is impossible to reproduce the rhythms and musical qualities of Persian poetry in English translation. But working together, we have arranged some translations to be recited with musical accompaniment, in conjunction with the original versions in Persian. In the case of quatrains, Sabrineh recites the poems in Persian with a light musical accompaniment offered by David on the Persian *setar,* an instrument long associated with Sufi mystical poetry. After the presentation in Persian, David offers the work in English. This way of presenting the poems works well, allowing listeners to get a taste of the Persian originals in addition to the translations in English. As a collaboration between a native speaker of Persian and a native speaker of English, these performances, like our translations, build a bridge between cultures, while the poems highlight deeper and timeless aspects of human spirituality.

In our work of translation, we pay a great deal of attention to finding just the right phrasing for the lines in English. An effective poem often possesses the quality of an *incantation,* something literally "suffused with song." This is the very quality missing in literal translations that makes them precise but "flat." Even if not performed or recited, our translations are meant—at the very least—to be heard within the mind's ear, and not simply read. In this way, owing to careful attention to their phrasing, the translations possess an internal rhythm, momentum, and structure—even in the case of the short, four-line *rubāʿiyāt.*

Recordings of original Persian poems with translation can be accessed on our website at www.sufipoetry.com.

Stringing Pearls:
The Forms of Persian Poetry

All classical Persian poetry is carefully structured in terms of rhyme, meter, and form. This appendix explains the basic structure and rhyme scheme of the three poetic forms most used by classical Sufi poets: the *rubāʿī* (quatrain), the *ghazal* (ode), and the *mathnawī* (couplet).

In the original Persian, the rhythmic, songlike quality of the *rubāʿī* and *ghazal* forms has an intoxicating effect, which inspired the use of this poetry at Sufi gatherings.

THE RUBĀʿī, OR QUATRAIN

A *rubāʿī* is a four-line poem that follows the rhyme scheme *a-a-b-a.* (In some cases, though, all lines rhyme.) Because they are so short, quatrains tend to be aphoristic, even epigrammatic. In some quatrains the first two lines make a statement, the third line provides an antithesis, and the fourth line provides a synthesis, resolution, or summary of the entire poem. Along with their rhythm and rhyme, Persian quatrains almost always embody a "rhythm of ideas," which contributes to their aphoristic and musical nature.

The *rubāʿī* form arose in the Persian province of Khorasan, which was also the birthplace of Persian Sufism. According to tradition, the great Sufi master Abū Saʿīd Abī 'l-Khayr (967–1049) was the first person to introduce the use of poetry—and specifically the quatrain—into Sufi practice. Quatrains were used as a way to summarize complex ideas in a nutshell, both in talks and in writings. In addition to summarizing teachings, quatrains were used to express devotional sentiments and to provide what one writer calls "a haiku-like encapsulation of a mystical state."

Each line of a quatrain is between ten and thirteen syllables long, and, like all Persian poetry, makes use of specific meters. (See form 1, pages 184–85.)

THE GHAZAL, OR ODE

The word *ghazal* means "words exchanged between lovers." *Ghazals* were originally love poems (or love songs) and maintained that emphasis after being adopted by the Sufis.

An ideal length for a *ghazal* is sometimes considered to be around seven lines; these poems can be considerably longer, though usually not more than fifteen lines. Like quatrains, *ghazals* use a monorhyme: each complete verse in the poem ends with the same sound or patterns of sound, and the first two half-verses rhyme as well. (See sample 2, pages 186–87.) The first major Sufi poet to leave us a collection of *ghazals* is Sanā'ī (d. 1131), one of the first great Sufi poets.

Persian poets referred to their craft as "stringing pearls"; that is, each complete poem is a necklace composed of individual pearls, or verses. An interesting feature of the *ghazal* is that each "pearl" or verse stands as an independently complete poetic thought. If the first and final lines of the poem are left in place, it is often possible to rearrange the position of the other "pearls" in the poem, without affecting its overall meaning.

Another feature of the *ghazal* is the common mention of the poet's pen name (*takhalluṣ*) in the final line or lines. Rather than being a signature in the modern sense, the pen name is used as a formal way to close the poem.

Rūmī was a prolific composer of *ghazals*. He never used his own name but often invoked that of "Shams of Tabriz"—his spiritual mentor—in closing his poems. Rūmī's collection of *ghazals*, the *Dīwān-i Shams-i Tabrīzī* (The Collected Poems of Shams of Tabriz), is staggering in its scope; it contains over 3,200 *ghazals* and close to 1,700 quatrains.

THE MATHNAWĪ, OR RHYMED COUPLET

In the *mathnawī* form (pronounced *masnavī* in Persian), each half-verse making up a complete verse rhymes. (See sample 3, pages 188–89.) Unlike the *rubāʿī* and *ghazal* forms (which use a monorhyme throughout the entire poem), the rhyme is allowed to change with each line. This made it possible for poets to use the *mathnawī* form for writing very lengthy works and specifically encouraged Sufi poets to use the *mathnawī* form for longer "teaching works."

The first Sufi poet to use the *mathnawī* form was Sanā'ī, in his wide-ranging work, *The Garden of Truth*. This was followed by 'Aṭṭār's epic work, *The Conference of the Birds*. Rūmī's students encouraged him to compose a similar teaching work, like those of Sanā'ī and 'Aṭṭār. The result is considered one of the hallmark works of Persian Sufism, commonly known simply as the *Mathnawī*, spanning six books and about twenty-five thousand verses.

Rūmī's *Mathnawī* begins with the famous "Song of the Reed Flute"; below we have reproduced the first few lines of that prologue to illustrate the rhyme scheme of the *mathnawī* form.

Many other types of Persian poetry exist, including the *qaṣīda* (eulogy) and the *qiṭ'a* (fragment). Yet nearly all Sufi poetry follows the three primary forms outlined in this appendix.

SAMPLES OF THE THREE FORMS

The following pages contain a sample of each of the three forms. The Persian version appears on each left-hand page, while the English translation appears on the right. In each sample we have highlighted the rhyme patterns of the Persian text in bold. Audio files of these samples, read in Persian, can be accessed on our website at www.sufipoetry.com.

1 bingar bi-jahān sirr-i ilāhī **pinhān**

2 chun āb-i ḥayāt dar siyāhī **pinhān**

3 paydā āmad zi baḥr māhī anbūh

4 shud baḥr zi anbūhī-yi m**āhī pinhān**

FORM 1 RUBĀ'Ī, OR QUATRAIN:
The Secret Is Hidden by Abū Sa'īd Abī 'l-Khayr

A *rubā'ī* is a four-line poem following a specific meter, in which lines one, two, and four follow the same rhyme pattern. In the example above, not only does the final word (*pinhān*, "hidden") rhyme, but so too does the last part of the previous word (*-āhī*).

1 Look at the world:
   the Divine Secret is hidden.

2 Like the Fountain of Life,
   it's hidden in darkness.

3 Millions of fish
   appeared in the sea—

4 Because of their number,
   the sea went into hiding.

1 dar miyān-i pardah-i khūn 'ishq rā gulz**ārhā**
  'āshiqān rā bā jamāl-i 'ishq-i bī chūn k**ārhā**

2 'aql gūyad shish jihat ḥaddast u bīrūn rāh nīst
  'ishq gūyad rāh hast u raftah'am man b**ārhā**

3 'aql bāzārī bidīd u tājirī āghāz kard
  'ishq dīdah zān sūy bāzār-i ū bāz**ārhā**

4 ay basā manṣūr-i pinhān zi'timād-i jān-i 'ishq
  tark-i minbarhā biguftah bar shudah bar d**ārhā**

5 'āshiqān-i durd kish rā dar darūna dhawqhā
  'āqilān-i tīrah dil rā dar darūn ink**ārhā**

6 'aql gūyad pā manih kandar fanā juz khār nīst
  'ishq gūyad 'aql rā kandar tu ast ān kh**ārhā**

7 hīn khamush kun khār-i hastī rā zi pā-yi dil bikan
  tā bibīnī dar darūn-i khwīshtan gulz**ārhā**

8 Shams-i Tabrīzī tu'ī khūrshīd andar abr-i ḥarf
  chūn bar āmad āftābat maḥw shud guft**ārhā**

FORM 2 GHAZAL, OR ODE:
Rose Gardens of the Heart by Rūmī

Each complete verse of a *ghazal* follows the same rhyme pattern, as does each half-verse of the first line.

1 The rose gardens of love are hidden in the heart;
  lovers are always doing business with Incomparable
    Beauty.

2 Reason said, "We live in a world of six directions—
    and that's it."
  Love replied, "There is a path beyond, and I have
    traveled it many times."

3 Reason saw a market and set up shop,
  but love trades in another currency altogether.

4 Oh! Trusting in love's essence, many hidden souls
  have left reason's pulpit and faced the gallows like
    Ḥallāj!

5 Lovers who drink the dregs are full of knowledge and
    joy;
  but intellectuals, dark in heart, are full of denial.

6 Reason said, "The pathway of selflessness is nothing
    but thorns."
  Love replied, "Those thorns are inside yourself."

7 But now, be silent—
  Clear away those thorns from the depths of your
    heart.
  Then you'll see the rose gardens within.

8 Shams of Tabrīz, you are the sun melting away the
    fog of empty talk.
  Since your sun rose, all that has vanished.

1 bishnū az nay chūn ḥikāyat **mīkunad**
  az judā'īhā shikāyat **mīkunad**

2 kaz nayistān tā marā bubrīdah'**and**
  dar nafīram mard u zan nālīdah'**and**

3 sīnah khwāham sharḥah sharḥah az firāq
  tā bigūyam sharḥ-i dard-i ishtiyāq

4 har kasī kū dūr mānd az aṣl-i **khwīsh**
  bāz jūyad rūzgār-i waṣl-i **khwīsh**

FORM 3 MATHNAWĪ, OR RHYMED COUPLET:
Song of the Reed Flute by Rūmī

In the *mathnawī* form, each half-verse rhymes, and the rhyme changes
with each new verse.

1 *Listen to the reed flute,*
  its song of separation:

2 Ever since I was cut from the reed-bed,
  men and women have moaned from my sound.

3 I need a heart torn by separation,
  so you may understand the pain of love's desire.

4 Whoever's been taken from his home
  always wishes to return.

Glossary

Annihilation (*fanā'*). "Passing away" or loss of the normal sense of the self, which enables the mystic to experience the presence of God. Usually paired with *baqā'* ("permanence" or "abiding"). By passing away from the ego, the mystic discovers the true self that abides.

Attributes (*ṣifāt*). The multiple qualities of God that are expressed in creation and are related to the names (*asmā'*) of God. For example, the attribute of mercy is reflected in the name "the Merciful." While the names and attributes may be described, the essence (*dhāt*) of God is beyond description. *See also* Essence and Most Beautiful Names.

Beloved. Also "the Friend." A common Sufi name for God as the object of love and spiritual desire. Can also be used to denote a human being who mirrors divine attributes.

Completed Human (*al-insān al-kāmil*). An individual who comes to reflect all levels of existence and all the divine names. Often translated "Perfect Man," the idea first appears in the writings of Ibn al-'Arabī. The completed human being lies latent within each person but needs to be realized.

Day of Alast. In pre-eternity, when souls were created, God asked, *Alastu bi-rabbikum*, "Am I not your Lord?" They replied, "Yes, we affirm that!" (Qur'ān 7:171). In Sufi interpretation, this exchange established the essential covenant between God and those souls. During this banquet, before the creation of the world, those souls drank the wine of pre-eternity with God. The ability to remember this event returns a soul to its primordial state of surrender to the divine.

Dervish (*darwīsh*). Literally, "one who waits at the threshold." A follower of the Sufi path; one who strives for spiritual poverty or emptiness.

Ego (*nafs*). The lower, impulsive self that needs to be purified. Used in this sense, *nafs* refers to the *nafs al-ammārah*, "the compulsive self" or "the commanding self." In some schools of Sufi thought, there is a ladder of "selves" or more refined levels of awareness, such as "the inspired self," "the contented self," and others. One goal of Sufi training is to purify the ego and gain access to these more refined states of awareness.

Essence (*dhāt*). The most essential, innermost, and unified dimension of something, which is beyond description. In the case of God, essence is contrasted with attributes (*ṣifāt*) and names.

Friend. *See* Beloved.

Idol. In a negative sense, anything that stands between an individual and God. In an opposite, ironic sense, "idol" can also refer to the Beloved or God.

Ka'ba. The cubic structure at Mecca, covered with a black cloth, that is the destination of pilgrimage and marks the direction of prayer (*qibla*) for Muslims. According to tradition, it was originally established by Adam and rebuilt by Abraham and his son Ishmael. In the time of the Prophet Muḥammad, the Ka'ba had been filled with idols by the tribes of Arabia. By removing the 360 idols, Muḥammad reestablished the Ka'ba as a symbol of monotheism and Divine Unity.

Knowledge. Sufis differentiate between acquired, rational knowledge (*'ilm*) and mystical knowledge (*ma'rifa*). The term used by Persian writers for mystical knowledge is *'irfān*, and one who possesses such knowledge is an *'ārif*—a gnostic, mystic, or Sufi.

Mirror. A Sufi symbol of the human heart, which when polished and purified from the rust of egoism reflects the light of God. Other important "mirrors" include human nature in general (Adam, the archetype of humanity, was created in the image of God) and the universe, in which the attributes of the divine are reflected.

Most Beautiful Names (*al-asmā' al-ḥusnā*). According to the Qur'ān, "to Him belong the Most Beautiful Names." These names, traditionally numbered at ninety-nine, denote divine attributes and include such titles as "the Merciful," "the Living," "the Loving," "the Light," and so on. Allāh, the Supreme Name, is not included in the list.

Moth. The lover drawn to the light of the Beloved. The moth's sacrifice of itself in the candle's flame is an instance of annihilation under the spell of love.

Oneness (*tawḥīd*). "Divine Unity." The acceptance and affirmation of the Oneness of God. The most central belief in Islam, for Sufis it usually leads to a belief in the Unity of Being (*see below*).

Permanence (*baqā'*). "Remaining," "abiding," or "subsistence." After the passing away of the conditioned self in annihilation, *baqā'* is the discovery of the abiding, permanent quality of the true self, which exists through God. The term entered Sufism from the Qur'ān, 55:26:

"All on earth will pass away, but the Face of the Lord will remain forever."

Posteternity (*abad*). Eternity without end. For some Sufis, posteternity is another name for permanence, or *baqā'*. *See also* pre-eternity.

Prayer niche (*miḥrāb*). The heart-shaped arch in a mosque that indicates the direction of prayer, facing the Ka'ba. In Sufi poetry, the arch of the beloved's eyebrow often becomes the *miḥrāb*.

Pre-eternity (*azal*). Eternity without beginning: that which exists before the creation of time and the world, pre-eternity is often coupled with posteternity (*abad*). The relationship between pre-eternity and posteternity is analogous to the relationship between annihilation and permanence.

The Real (*al-ḥaqq*). Ultimate Reality, or "the Truth." One of the most common names for God and the divine level of reality in Sufi literature.

Rind. A "spiritual libertine" or "rogue." Impossible to translate with a single word, a *rind* is liberated from outward social conventions but inwardly possesses a saint-like nature that is beyond reproach.

Samā'. "Spiritual Audition" or the "Spiritual Concert." A practice during Sufi gatherings that employs music and the recitation of poetry as a form of mystical remembrance of the divine. Sometimes movement or dance is involved, as in the turning of the whirling dervishes.

The Sea. Absolute being and unity.

Sufi. A follower of the mystic path who seeks purification of the self and experiential knowledge of the divine.

Tavern (*kharābāt*). The place of "ruins"; the gathering place where spiritual wine is served to *rinds* or Sufis.

Two Worlds. This world and the next. The phrase "the two worlds" is commonly used in Sufi poetry to denote everything that exists.

Unity of Being. The teaching of Ibn al-ʿArabī (1165–1240) that the entire universe, and everything that exists, is a manifestation of God. This does not mean that the universe is God, but that everything manifested is an aspect of God's existence.

Veil. In the same way that the divine is mirrored in the world, it is also veiled and hidden. One of the terms for coming to know God directly is "unveiling" (*kashf*). There is also an Islamic belief that if all the veils of manifestation were lifted, a person gazing directly on the face of God would be annihilated.

Water of Life. Located in darkness, the Fountain of Life is associated with the mysterious figure Khiḍr, the Islamic "Green Man" — a cross between a prophet, saint, and bestower of spiritual initiations. Khiḍr achieved immortality from the Fountain of Life.

Wine. Overwhelming love.

World-viewing Cup. A miraculous cup, like a magic mirror, that allows its possessor to see the entire world by gazing into its depths. According to legend, it was possessed by the ancient Persian king Jam. In Sufi symbolism, it is associated with the purified heart.

Notes

p. 3, INVISIBLE CARAVANS | *Love's concert is calling, but the flute can't be seen*: literally, "All men are in *samā'*, but the flute can't be seen." For *samā'*, see glossary.

p. 5, THE SAME LANGUAGE | Excerpt from Rūmī, *Mathnawī* I, 1205–1207.

p. 7, STONE HEARTS | *the Spiritual Concert:* literally, *samā'*.

p. 13, THE GLOW OF YOUR PRESENCE | Excerpt from Ḥāfiẓ, *Ghazal* 22.

p. 14, EVERY DIRECTION | *why aim your prayers at only one spot?*: a reference to the *qibla,* the direction of prayer at Mecca.

p. 17, THE PATHWAY FINALLY OPENED | *freed from both belief and from disbelief*: belief and disbelief can both be seen as forms of idolatry. The idea that God is beyond belief and disbelief is a common theme in Sufi mystical poetry.

p. 18, THE KING'S ROYAL FALCON | *daring*: in Persian, *jānbāz*, "reckless" or "willing to risk one's life."

p. 21, THE SUFI'S CAP | Excerpt from Sa'dī, *Gulistān*, book 2, story 15. *What's the use of those woolen robes and the Sufi's cloak?*: for some dervishes, the patched robe (*khirqa*) and other types of clothing worn by initiates became sources of spiritual pride.

p. 22, ESSENCE AND FORM | In the original Persian, this is a very abstract, metaphysical poem, in which the divine essence (*dhāt*) is contrasted with the attributes (*ṣifāt*). The last line of our translation is literal, and the other lines convey the sense of the original. For *essence* and *attributes*, see glossary.

p. 25, THE GREATEST NAME | *We are the Treasure whose spell is the world*: in a traditional Sufi saying God said, "I was a hidden treasure who wished to be known, so I created the world." The word we have translated as "spell" is *ṭilism* or "talisman," a magical image or charm.
| *The Greatest Name* (*ism-i a'ẓam*) or the Supreme Name: Allāh.

The poem expresses the view that humanity—Adam— was made in the image of God and is a mirror of the divine essence and attributes. The poet, Maghribī, was influenced by the ideas of Ibn al-'Arabī.

p. 28, REALITY AND APPEARANCE | *There is a difference between real love and the love of appearances*: literally, "there is a difference between real love (*'ishq-i ḥaqīqī*) and metaphorical love (*'ishq-i majāzī*)." The meaning of this is that there is a difference between divine love for God and "metaphorical love" for a human being. At the same time, the Sufis maintained that human love can be a direct gateway to love of the divine. As the saying goes, "The apparent is a bridge to the Real." See Annemarie Schimmel, *As Through a Veil: Mystical Poetry in Islam* (Oxford: One World, 2001), pp. 68–69.

p. 29, HUNDREDS OF WAYS | *There are hundreds of ways to kneel in prayer — hundreds of ways to open toward the heart of the Friend's beauty*: literally, "There are a hundred kinds of prayer (*nāmāz*), bowing (*rukū'*), and prostration (*sujūd*) for the one whose prayer niche (*miḥrāb*) is the beauty of the Friend."

p. 33, THE WIND AT DAWN | *From before-the-beginning to beyond-the-last*: for *pre-eternity* and *posteternity*, see glossary.

p. 34, NOT WHAT WE THOUGHT | *The Water of Life is in this very house — but still, we need to drink it*: literally, "That Fountain from which Khiḍr drank the Water of Life is in our home, but we've bottled it up." For *water of life*, see glossary.

p. 37, ONE AND MANY | *The essence is one, but the attributes many*: see *essence* and *attributes* in glossary.

p. 38, REMEMBER THE TRUTH | *If you hear those two words, then remember the Truth*: literally, "if you hear those two words, then remember the ego" (and then remember the Truth, by forgetting yourself).

p. 39, THIS SORROW | In Persian poetry, the term "sorrow" or "your sorrow" is often used for "love" or "your love," respectively.

p. 42, TAVERN DWELLERS | *The pure-hearted Sufis no longer care to exist*: literally, "The *rind* no longer inclines toward existence." For *rind*, see glossary.

p. 43, KNOWLEDGE | *The path of knowledge*: literally, "the path of *gnōsis*" (*ma'rifa*).

p. 46, THE HIDDEN SUN | *The heavenly spheres have lost their way in your amazement. Bewildered and wondering, they forever turn before your door.* 'Aṭṭār is describing how the

stars and the entire celestial sphere revolve around the one
point of the Pole Star. This beautiful passage parallels the
idea of some Greek philosophers that the movement of the
heavenly spheres is caused by their contemplation and desire
to return to the First Cause — and Dante's idea that love is
the power that moves the stars.

p. 47, THE HEART'S HOUSE | A free translation from Rūmī,
Mathnawī II, 3129–32.

p. 53, FIND IT IN YOU | *The Divine Book*: the creative pattern
from which the world is fashioned.

p. 54, LIFT THE VEIL | According to a tradition of Islamic
mysticism, "Were His face unveiled, the glories of His face
would burn whatever His vision reached."

p. 56, RUINED | *prayer niche* (see glossary). In Sufi poetry, the
curve of the beloved's eyebrow becomes the prayer niche.

p. 59, WITHOUT YOU | *celestial lake*: literally, *Kawthar*, a river
or fountain of paradise mentioned once in the Qur'ān
(108:1); it means "abundance."

p. 60, SERVICE | Not a poem, but a famous saying from Saʿdī's
Bustān, book 1, story 5.

p. 61, THE MISSING SUN | This poem probably refers to the
absence of Shams of Tabriz; *Shams* means "sun" in Arabic.
The term *circle of love* means "the circle of dervishes."

p. 62, WE WERE TOGETHER | Here *idol* refers to God, and *we
can't exist without him* is a clever pun.
| *that ancient Night of Union*: the primordial banquet of
The Day of *Alast* (see glossary), when souls established their
covenant with God. From that wine drunk in
preexistence, "before the grape was created," the souls are
drunk until the end of time.

p. 63, BEYOND DISTINCTIONS | *belief and disbelief*: see note to
the poem "The Pathway Finally Opened," p. 199.
| *Love's Prophet is beyond race, beyond creeds, beyond petty
distinctions*: literally, "Love's Prophet is neither Persian nor
Arab."

p. 66, CHECKMATE | This poem, by a twentieth-century Persian
poet, shows the abiding influence of the Sufi tradition.
References to the game of chess were often made in classical
Sufi poetry.

p. 68, TAKE A LOOK THERE | *People of Heart*: a name for Sufis.

p. 71, THE VISION OF YOUR FACE | *Your love, from before the
beginning of time*: that is, from *azal*, or pre-eternity. This
poem by Sulṭān Walad (1226–1312), the son of Jalāl al-Dīn
Rūmī, is a recollection of gazing on the face of the Beloved
before the creation of the world.

p. 72, THE MIRROR AND ITS CASE | *Each soul is created to serve
as your mirror*: literally, "The purpose of the existence
of humanity and the jinn is a mirror." The Qur'ān states
that human beings and the jinn were created for the sole
purpose of worshiping God (51:56). One of the companions
of the Prophet, 'Abdallāh Ibn 'Abbās, explained that the
word *worship*, in this case, means "to know God." The jinn
are genies, inhabitants of the subtle world.

p. 76, ACTION | The image of an ass who carries a load of books
but doesn't benefit from them appears in the Qur'ān 62:5.

p. 77, TRADING IN LOVE'S CURRENCY | Excerpt from Rūmī,
Ghazal 132; the complete *ghazal* appears in appendix 2.

p. 78, THE BUBBLE | *Pass away* and *eternal shore*: *fanā'*
and *baqā'*, respectively. For *annihilation* and *permanence*, see
glossary.

p. 82, THE SUN AND THE SHADOW | *erased*: *maḥw*, another term for *fanā'*.

p. 87, BETWEEN TWO BREATHS | The author of this quatrain, the famous philosopher-scientist Avicenna (980–1037), was also the author of several spiritual allegories about the journey of the soul.

p. 89, DON'T IMAGINE | *wayfarer*: Arabic, *sālik*; a "traveler" on the spiritual path; a Sufi.

p. 90, DON'T UTTER A SOUND | *nightingale*: a symbol of the lover, drawn to the rose of the Beloved. In the same way that the flame draws the moth to it, the eternal beauty of the rose attracts the nightingale and inspires it to song. While the moth ignores the danger of the flame, the nightingale ignores the danger of the thorns.

p. 92, YOUR GENEROSITY | *who needs to ask the sun* [shams] *for its light?* An allusion to Shams of Tabriz.

p. 101, CREATION MYTH | *Made moist with love's dew, Adam's soil became clay*: according to the Qur'ān, Adam was molded out of clay (or matter) and imbued with the spirit (*rūh*) of God. For the Persian poets, the word *Adam* also means "humankind."

p. 104, EVERY PLACE IS LOVE'S HOME | Excerpt from Ḥāfiẓ, Ghazal 78.

p. 106, BURNT | Nothing is known about the author, but his name, Qīrī, appropriately enough, means "hot tar."

p. 108, THE SECRET IS HIDDEN | *the Divine Secret is hidden*: the secret (*sirr*) is also hidden in the human being. In Sufi teachings, the *sirr* is the innermost awareness in the heart, which is a human being's link with the divine.
| *Like the Fountain of Life, it's hidden in darkness*: see glossary, *water of life*. The Fountain of Life was said to

reside in a "dark land." According to one account, it was located in the north, under the Pole Star, where the sun doesn't rise. When a dead, salted fish fell into the water, it sprang back to life and helped Khiḍr to discover the Fountain of Life. In this way, "the Water of Life arrived unsought."

p. 112, DUST ON YOUR DOORSTEP | Ḥāfiẓ, excerpt from Ghazal 34. *My soul is just the dust on your doorstep*: the phrase "dust on your doorstep," common in Ḥāfiẓ and other poets, denotes the ultimate spiritual surrender of the lover. According to one definition, "Sufism is to stay at the door of the Beloved even if you are driven away." The doorway is a threshold to another way of perception.

p. 119, SEEKING YOU TOO | *on the very first day*: in pre-eternity, before the creation of the world.
| *with true promise*: the Persian word translated as "promise" is *paymān*, which also means "treaty" or "covenant." This one word supplies a key to the entire poem, showing that it's about the Day of Alast (see glossary) or the "day of covenant."
| *O Seeker!* A play on the name of the poet, who is being addressed here. His name, Ṭālib, means "seeker."

p. 125, ACHIEVE THE STATE | *you must move from speech to the inner state. You won't become one just by chanting "Unity"*: this poem may be a critique of the Sufi meditative practice of repeating divine names in Arabic using a rosary (*tasbīḥ*). As long as it involves repeating words without a change in spiritual state (*ḥāl*), the practice remains questionable.

p. 132, THE MIRROR AND THE SUN | A literal translation of the second half of the quatrain: *At that moment when the sun shines at the mirror, if the mirror does not say "I am the sun," what else should it do?* This is almost certainly a reference to the fate of Manṣūr al-Ḥallāj (857–922). In a moment of mystical ecstasy and effacement, he uttered the line "I am the Truth" (*al-ḥaqq*, "the Real," a name of God), for which he was put to death.

p. 133, FACES | *human beings are the face of God*: the "face" is the most intimate aspect of something. In Islamic mysticism, "Adam"—humanity—is made in God's image, mirroring the essence and attributes of the divine.

p. 134, TAKE A CLOSER LOOK | *The Real said to you, "I'm wherever you turn"—So why don't you take a closer look at yourself?* Qur'ān 2:115: "Wherever you turn, there is the face of God."

p. 137, THE WORLD-VIEWING CUP | See glossary.

p. 140, KEEP ME FREE | *forget the wine and the cup*: literally, "I am free from wine and cup."
| *let's sell the farm*: literally, "I am free from seed and trap."

p. 142, EMPTINESS | *"when poverty becomes complete, you find God"*: an Arabic saying quoted by Sufi writers.

p. 144, IT WOULD BE ME | *Crazy yet learned—Scoundrel yet saint*: This poem celebrates the idea of the *rind*, or "spiritual libertine": one who has become free of social conventions but remains spiritually pure within.

p. 145, SILENCE | *Drink the wine of mystic knowledge, but don't then forget to keep your lips closed. It's never a good time to sell the Divine Secret!*: when Manṣūr al-Ḥallāj said *Anā al-ḥaqq*—I am the Real—he uttered the divine secret.

p. 148, BLIND AS A BAT | *Divine Oneness: tawḥīd*. For *oneness*, see glossary.

p. 149, Lost in Celebration | *we are now victorious in love!*: literally, "we are victorious." A play on the name of Manṣūr al-Ḥallāj—*manṣūr* means "victorious."

p. 156, Without Your Presence | Excerpt from Ḥāfiẓ, Ghazal 29.

p. 160, Sweep Out the Stable | *Sweep out the stable of your existence and the king will gladly enter*: literally, "sweep out the *khargāh* (tent or pavilion) of your existence." We have translated *khargāh* as "stable" because of its resonance with the Persian word for donkey (*khar*).

p. 161, Creation's Witness | An elaboration on the Islamic mystical saying "I was a Hidden Treasure that wished to be known, so I created the world."

p. 167, One Body | This poem by Saʿdī (*Gulistān*, book 1, story 10) is inscribed at the entrance to the Hall of Nations at the United Nations building in New York.

p. 171, Clear Wine | *Most Beautiful Names*: see glossary.

p. 173, Be Like the Ocean | Quatrain and line of commentary from Saʿdī, *Gulistān*, book 2, story 40.

Index of Authors

Because quatrains were widely quoted by Sufi authors but rarely "signed" by the original writer, some quatrains "wander" throughout collections of Sufi literature and are attributed to more than one author. Biographical information about the more well-known writers can be found in John Renard's *Historical Dictionary of Sufism* (Lanham, MD: Scarecrow Press, 2005). When known, years for the death of the more well-known authors are given using European, common era dates, though some dates are approximate. For sources of the individual poems, see the translators' website.

About the Translators

David Fideler has worked as an editor, publisher, college professor, educational consultant, and the program director of a humanities center. He gives presentations on Sufi poetry and holds a PhD in philosophy and cultural studies.

Sabrineh Fideler was born in Tehran and holds a degree in English to Persian translation from Azad University. Now living in the United States, she previously worked as a freelance translator for Iran University Press.

David and Sabrineh currently live in West Michigan.

HELPING TO PRESERVE OUR ENVIRONMENT

New World Library uses 100% postconsumer-waste recycled paper for our books whenever possible, even if it costs more. During 2008 this choice saved the following precious resources:

46,104 trees were saved

www.newworldlibrary.com

ENERGY	WASTEWATER	GREENHOUSE GASES	SOLID WASTE
32 MILLION BTU	17 MILLION GAL.	4 MILLION LB.	2 MILLION LB.

Environmental impact estimates were made using the Environmental Defense Fund Paper Calculator @ www.papercalculator.org.